D0359127

Religious Signs and Symbols

Christianity

Cath Senker

WAYLAND

First published in 2008 by Wayland

Copyright © Wayland 2008

Illustrations copyright © Emmanuel Cerisier,
Christopher Corr, Roberto Tomei

Wayland
338 Euston Road
London NW1 3BH

Wayland Australia
Level 17/207 Kent Street
Sydney, NSW 2000

All rights reserved

Senior editor: Camilla Lloyd
Consultant: Anita Ganeri
Designer: Phipps Design
Illustrators: Emmanuel Cerisier: Cover (front and
back), 7, 13, 29, 32;
Christopher Corr: 1, 5, 8, 11, 31;
Roberto Tomei: 2, 9, 21
Picture researcher: Kathy Lockley

British Library Cataloguing in Publication Data:
Senker, Cath
    Christianity. - (Religious signs and symbols)
    1. Christian art and symbolism - Juvenile literature
    I. Title
    246

ISBN: 978 0 7502 5332 1

Printed in China

Wayland is a division of Hachette Children's Books,
an Hachette Livre UK company
www.hachettelivre.co.uk

Picture Acknowledgments: The author and publisher
would like to thank the following for their pictures to
be reproduced in this publication: Cover illustrations:
Emmanuel Cerisier (both); ArkReligion.com/Alamy:
10, 14, 22; Bernadette Delaney/Alamy: 23; Chris
Fairclough: 6 (both), 12, 15, 16, 19; Con Tanasiuk/
Design Pictures/Corbis: 24; Image Source/Corbis: 4;
Jenny Matthews/Alamy: 20; Mike Theiss/Ultimate
Chase/Corbis: 5; Oswald Rivas/Reuters/Corbis: 26;
Sebastian Pfuetze/zefa/Corbis: 18.

WORCESTERSHIRE COUNTY COUNCIL	
949	
Bertrams	09/10/2008
J230	£12.99
WS	

With special thanks to Sam Dilkes.

The author and publisher would like to thank the following models: Celine Clark, Isobel
Grace, Hari Johal and Charlie Pengelly.

Acknowledgments:
The author would like to thank the following for permission to reproduce material in this
book: p.9 Snowman Poem, by Maureen Spell; p.17 Communion bread recipe from Cooks.com;
p.21 Story from County Clare Folk-Tales and Myths by Thomas Johnson Westropp, County
Clare Library; p.23 Song from Christian Songs for Children, Sowerby Bridge, England (Sheet
and instrumental music available from http://patamb.supanet.com/lambs/Communion.html);
p.29 Story adapted from The Symbolism of the Ukrainian Easter egg.
www.uazone.net/holidays/EasterEggs.html

Note: Please ask an adult to help you with the recipes and activities in this book.

Every effort has been made by the author to clear copyright for the items in this edition.
Should there be any inadvertent omission please apply to the publisher for rectification.

Contents

Activities

There are lots of activities throughout this book.

You can **read** stories, folk tales, holy stories, and poems on pages 7, 9, 11, 13, 15, 21, 29.

You can **sing** songs on page 23.

You can **make** traditional food on pages 17, 25.

You can **make** crafts and draw pictures on 5, 19, 27.

Signs and symbols

A sign usually has one clear meaning. There are examples of signs on the street. A 'stop' sign means just what it says!

A symbol can have many meanings. Think about the different meanings of a cross symbol. A cross can mean you have got a sum wrong. It can be a kiss that you write after you sign your name on a birthday card. The cross is also the most common Christian symbol.

This street sign has one clear meaning: no entry. Cars may not go down this street.

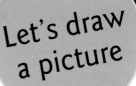

The cross

Think of different ways a cross can be used as a symbol. Draw pictures showing where you might find the symbol. Here are some examples.

The Red Cross

The Red Cross gives medical aid to people in wars. This symbol is on buildings and medical vehicles such as ambulances.

The Christian cross

The Latin Christian cross has a long stem. The Greek Christian cross has four equal arms.

A cross on a ballot paper

When people vote in elections, they vote for a person by marking the ballot (voting) paper with a cross.

The Christian Cross

Christians follow the teachings of Jesus. Jesus died on a cross. Christians believe that he died to save all of humankind. When Christians see a cross, it reminds them of Jesus.

Some Christians make the sign of the cross to **bless** themselves, other people or objects. They trace a cross on their body, from the forehead to the chest and from shoulder to shoulder. They make this blessing during prayer or in times of need or danger.

You often see a cross like this inside a church.

A crucifix shows the figure of Jesus.

The Three Trees

Once upon a time there were three trees on the top of a mountain. The first dreamt of being a treasure chest. The second wanted to be sailing ship. The third wanted to stay on the mountaintop, growing bigger and bigger.

One day, three woodcutters arrived. They chopped down the trees and sent them all away to different workshops. One became a feed box for animals in a stable. When baby Jesus was born, his mother placed him in that very feed box. The second tree became a little fishing boat. One stormy night, Jesus used it to shelter from a storm. The third was turned into a wooden beam – and became the cross on which Jesus died. From a simple beam, it became a worldwide symbol of the Christian religion.

The Holy Trinity

Christians believe there is one God who made the world. He is also three: the Father, the Son and the **Holy Spirit**. Christians call this the **Holy Trinity**.

God is the Father of Jesus, who is the Son. Christians believe that God is a perfect father. He loves and cares for his people, and protects them.

In Ireland St Patrick used the clover leaf with three leaves on one stem to explain the Trinity.

The Holy Spirit is God's power working in the world. The Holy Spirit is like the wind. You cannot see it but you can feel it, and it is powerful.

Trinity poem

When you see a snowman
Three snowballs round,
He is reminding you
That in God Three in One are found.

The bottom reminds us of God the
*   Father,*
Our strong rock and foundation
The Creator of all living things,
People, tribes and nations.

The middle shows us God the Son
With His arms spread open wide.
Who died on the cross for each of us
Our sins Jesus' blood did hide.

The head reminds us of God the
*   Holy Spirit*
Who is our counsellor [adviser] and
*   friend,*
He speaks to our hearts and minds
Transforming us in the likeness of
*   Him.*

So when you see a snowman
In the midst of all the wintertime fun,
Listen carefully and he'll tell you,
'Remember God is Three in One'.

By Maureen Spell

The fish

The first Christians lived under Roman rulers. The Romans **persecuted** them because they did not worship Roman gods. Sometimes they rounded up Christians and put them to death.

The fish symbol is still used today. Some Christians have a car bumper sticker with the symbol on it.

The Christians followed their faith in secret. They used the fish symbol as a secret sign to recognise each other.

Christians also believed there was a secret message in the Greek word for fish, *ixthus*. The six letters are the first letters of the words Jesus, Christ, God, Son and **Saviour** in Greek.

The origin of the fish symbol

In the days of the early Church, Christians had to hide their faith from the Romans. They needed a secret symbol so they would know if another person was a Christian and could be trusted. The fish was an obvious choice. Many Bible verses mentioned fish, and a fish was quick and simple to draw. To make the secret symbol, one person casually made an arc with their toe on the earth. If the other person was a Christian, he or she drew another arc to complete the fish drawing. Then the two could speak openly without fear.

The Bible

The Christian Bible includes the holy books of the Jews and the Christians. It contains many symbols that help people to understand God. For example, mountains stand for strong kingdoms. Hills stand for less powerful kingdoms. Valleys stand for the poor and humble. What might the symbols in this Bible verse mean?

'Every valley shall be filled, and every mountain and hill shall be made low.'
(Isaiah 40:4)

It could mean that the kingdoms will be brought down and the ordinary people lifted up, so that all are equal.

A Christian boy reads his children's Bible at bedtime.

Noah's Ark

*God created a beautiful world. After a while though, he saw that people were acting badly. They were fighting, stealing and telling lies. The only good people were Noah and his family. God decided to destroy everyone on earth, except for Noah's family. He told Noah to build an **ark** to save his family and a pair of every kind of animal. It was a long and tiring job building the ark and loading on all the animals. At last it was done.*

Soon after, God sent a flood to cover the earth and kill every living thing. Only Noah's family and the animals on the Ark were saved. When the rain finally stopped, Noah sent a dove to find land. It returned with an olive branch, showing that the floods had gone down and the land was dry. The dove was a symbol of the Holy Spirit and of peace – a symbol that God had ended his war with the human race.

Light

Light stops darkness and helps living things. For Christians, it is a symbol of God's presence.

It is also a symbol for Jesus. In church, people light one single candle to remind them of Jesus, who is the light of the world. They place two candles on the **altar** to stand for Jesus' human and godly natures.

A candle is also a symbol of prayer. Roman **Catholics** and **Orthodox Christians** light a candle before an image of Jesus or a saint and say a prayer.

At Easter, people light a candle called the Paschal candle, which stands for Jesus rising again after his death.

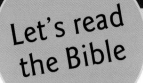

Bible verse

In this Bible verse, Jesus explains that being in the light means treating others well.

'I am the Light of the world.
He who follows Me shall not
walk in darkness,
But have the Light of Life.
He who says he is in the Light,

But hates his brother,
Is in darkness until now.
He who loves his brother abides [lives] in the Light,
And there is no cause for stumbling in him.

But he who hates his brother is in darkness
And walks in darkness,
And does not know where he is going,
Because the darkness has blinded his eyes.'

(John 8.12; 1 John 2.9–11)

Holy Communion and Eucharist

Eucharist, or **Mass** or **Holy Communion** for Roman Catholics, is the most important act of worship for many Christians. Eucharist means 'to give thanks'. At the Eucharist, people remember Jesus' **Last Supper** before he died.

This boy is taking Holy Communion in his church.

At the service, the **minister** blesses bread and wine. Everyone takes a small piece of bread and a sip of wine. The bread stands for the body of Jesus and the wine stands for his blood. It reminds Christians of what Jesus did for them. It is a way of thanking God for his gifts.

Let's make communion bread

Recipe for communion bread

Ask an adult to help you cook

You will need:

1 cup white flour
1 cup wholewheat flour
3/4 teaspoon salt
2 tablespoons melted butter
2 tablespoons honey
3/4 cup water

1. *Mix the wholewheat flour and salt in a large bowl and then add the butter, honey and water.*

2. *Beat the mixture with a wooden spoon until smooth, then add the white flour a little at a time. Beat it in until the dough is still soft but dry enough to handle.*

3. *Knead the dough by folding and punching it for 6 to 8 minutes until it is smooth and springy.*

4. *Make into circles roughly 15 cm (6 inches) in diameter and 1 cm (1/2 inch) thick.*

5. *Place the circles on a greased baking sheet. With a sharp knife, cut a criss-cross grid of lines 1 cm (1/2 inch) apart. Make sure the cuts are quite deep and go right to the edge.*

6. *Bake at 375° C (700° F) for 25 minutes or until the top is a light golden brown.*

7. *Cool on a wire rack before eating.*

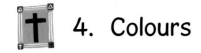

Meanings of colours

For Christians, colours have meanings. The cloths on the altar, **lectern** and **pulpit** and the minister's robes change according to the **cycles** of the Christian year. There is a Christmas cycle and an Easter cycle.

Within each cycle, these colours are used for the different times of the year:

Priests sometimes wear purple robes.

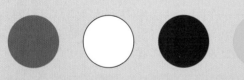

Purple: in the seasons preparing for a festival – **Advent** and **Lent**. Purple stands for fasting and asking forgiveness for doing wrong.

White: festivals of Easter, **Ascension Day** and Christmas. White stands for purity, light and celebration.

Red: **Holy Week** and **Whitsun** (Pentecost). Red stands for the Holy Spirit. At Whitsun Christians remember how Jesus' first followers became filled with the Holy Spirit. They gained the power to spread Jesus' teachings. Red is used during Holy Week to stand for the blood of Christ. A minister might also wear red robes.

Green: other times. It stands for growth in the Christian faith.

Let's draw a chart

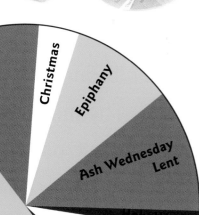

Pie chart of the church year

You will need:

Paper
A compass to draw a circle
Ruler
Colouring pencils

1. *Draw a circle on your paper.*

2. *Copy this pie chart below showing the church year.*

3. *Colour in the segments with the colours the church uses at that time of year.*

Advent

Christmas

Epiphany

Ash Wednesday
Lent

Holy Week

Easter Day
Easter
Ascension

Whitsun

Rest of the
church year

Baptism

Most Christians **baptise** babies with water. Baptism marks the start of a new life with God. During baptism, the minister sprinkles water on the baby's head. The water is a symbol that the baby is pure and clean. Because water is refreshing, it is also a symbol that baptism brings happiness to the baby.

A candle is lit to **symbolise** Jesus, who brought light to the world. The minister makes the sign of the cross on the baby's forehead to show he or she belongs to Christ. The parents and **godparents** promise that the baby will live life as a good Christian.

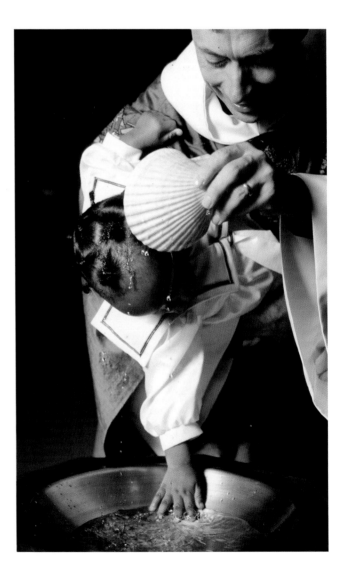

At the baptism, the baby wears white, which stands for purity

The baptism of Senán

In Moylough, County Clare in Ireland, a woman gave birth to a baby. One morning, when he was still tiny and not yet baptised, she was walking along with him. The woman was hungry and hadn't had time to prepare a meal. She stopped and ate some wild fruit to keep her going. 'You have an early appetite, mother', said the tiny baby. 'You have old talk, my child', she replied. She decided to name him Senán, from sean, meaning 'old'.

The mother now wanted to baptise her baby. Strangely for Ireland, which is a rainy country, there was no water at hand. Senán told his mother to pull up three rushes, and to her amazement, a lake appeared. Senán was baptised in the lake, which today is called Loughshanan. He grew up to become a great saint.

First Holy Communion and Confirmation

When children are old enough to understand what it means to be a Christian, they have their **confirmation**, or **First Holy Communion** if they are Catholics.

At both ceremonies, the **bishop** asks them questions about their beliefs, and they promise to live a good Christian life. The bishop places his hand on each child's head. It is a symbol of the strength that the Holy Spirit will bring the child. In a Catholic church, he draws the sign of the cross on the child's forehead. It is a sign of being chosen by God.

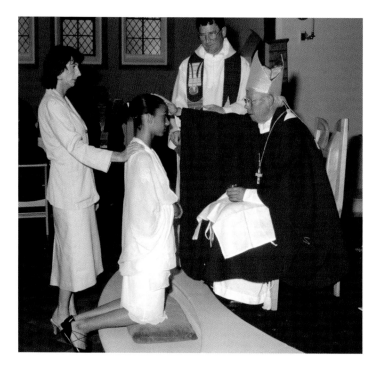

At the confirmation ceremony, the child wears white as a symbol of purity.

Let's sing a song

First Holy Communion Song

The waiting is over and this is the day
The nerves and the worries have all gone away
I'm ready to meet you in this special way
Come meet me, Lord Jesus, meet me
The bread and wine you offer free
Are symbols of your love for me
Come, sweet Jesus, meet me.

My teachers, my family, my friends and my priest
Have helped me prepare for the forthcoming feast
For all other things, I don't care in the least
Come meet me, Lord Jesus, meet me
Each and every day's been spent
Preparing for this sacrament [important religious ceremony]
Come, sweet Jesus, meet me.

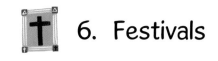

Preparing for Easter

During Lent, people prepare for Easter. Lent lasts for 40 days (not including Sundays) and ends on the day before Easter Sunday.

The day before Lent starts is **Shrove Tuesday**, a day of celebration. In the past, people did not eat meat, fish, fat, eggs or milky foods during Lent. They made pancakes to use up all the food that could not be eaten in Lent. Pancake Day is the symbol of this custom.

Christians go to church during Lent to ask for forgiveness for their sins.

Lent is a serious time. Christians remember how Jesus spent 40 days in the desert fasting and praying, while the devil tried to tempt him. They ask God to forgive them for things they have done wrong. Some people **fast** or give up their favourite foods to symbolise Jesus' suffering.

Recipe for pancake day

Ask an adult to help you cook

You will need:

100 g (4 oz) plain flour
1 large egg
300 ml (½ pint) milk
Pinch of salt

1. Sift the flour and pinch of salt into a mixing bowl and make a well in the middle.

2. Break the egg into the well. Whisk the egg so that it starts to mix with the flour from around the bowl.

3. Add the milk a little at a time. Mix everything together until the batter is smooth.

4. Heat a little butter in a frying pan.

5. Pour about 2–3 tablespoons of the mixture into the pan. Tilt and move the pan until the mixture covers the base evenly. Cook on a medium heat for 30–60 seconds until the pancake is golden. Flip it and cook on the other side.

6. Keep the pancake warm and repeat with the rest of the batter.

Palm Sunday

Holy Week is the week leading up to Easter Sunday. It is the most serious week of the Christian year.

Palm Sunday is the first day of Holy Week. Christians remember how Jesus entered Jerusalem on a donkey for the **Passover** feast. The crowds cheered him and laid palm leaves on the ground. This was how a king was welcomed in those days.

In memory of the story, worshippers carry palm leaves or home-made palm crosses. They go on a procession in and around the church.

A child waves palm crosses on the Palm Sunday procession.

Let's make a palm cross

Palm cross

You will need:

A4 sheet of card
Ruler
Pencil
Scissors
Stapler

1. Cut two strips of card 1.5 cm wide.

2. Make the crossbeam. On one strip, mark from the left 2 cm, 4 cm, 10 cm and 20 cm.

3. Fold from the right along the 20 cm and then the 10 cm line.

4. Turn the card over. Fold forward along the 2 cm and then the 4 cm line. This makes the centre of the crossbeam. Flatten the card.

5. Make the cross. Insert one end of the other strip of card under the top layer of the centre of the crossbeam.

6. Fold the long piece of card behind the crossbeam. Thread it up in front of it and then under the top layer of the centre of the crossbeam. Pull it through and flatten it.

7. Thread the long piece of card back under the centre of the crossbeam. Stop when a cross shape is made.

8. Secure your cross with a staple in the centre. Ask an adult to help you with the stapler. If you need help with this activity please see the websites on page 31.

Easter

On the Friday after Palm Sunday, the Roman rulers arrested Jesus and put him to death on the cross. Christians call this day Good Friday because Jesus showed his goodness by dying for the sake of humankind.

You can dip hard-boiled eggs in half a cup of water, 1 tablespoon of vinegar and food colouring. Let the eggs dry and you will have colourful eggs for Easter!

The Bible says that on the Sunday, Jesus rose from the dead. His followers were amazed to see him alive again.

On Easter Sunday, people remember this extraordinary event. They decorate Easter eggs and exchange chocolate eggs. Eggs are a symbol of new life. Christians believe that death is not the end. Jesus is still alive, with God in heaven. When people die, they too start a new life with God.

A Ukrainian folk tale

When Jesus was dying on the cross, blood flowing from his wounds fell on the ground. Wherever a drop fell, a red egg was created. Jesus' mother, Mary, was standing beneath his cross praying and crying. She gathered all the eggs into a handkerchief. Her tears turned the eggs into elaborate decorated Easter eggs.

Mary went to the ruler, Pontius Pilate, to ask if she could bury her son. On her way there, she gave an Easter egg to all the children she met, telling them to live in peace. When she arrived at the palace, she fainted and dropped the eggs. The Easter eggs rolled all over the world. Since then, people everywhere have decorated eggs at Easter as a symbol of love and peace.

Advent The period of four weeks before Christmas when people prepare for the festival. 'Advent' means 'coming'.

altar The holy table at the front of the church.

ark A huge boat that Noah built to save his family and animals from the flood.

Ascension Day The Thursday 40 days after Easter Sunday when Christians remember Jesus' ascension – when he rose up to heaven.

baptise To welcome a person into the church through a ceremony that involves water.

bishop The minister in charge of the churches in a large area called a diocese.

bless To ask God to protect someone or something.

Catholics People who are members of the part of the church that has the Pope as leader.

confirmation A ceremony in which people promise to be good Christians. It is called a confirmation because they confirm the promises that were made for them when they were baptised.

crucifix A model of a cross with a figure of Jesus Christ on it, as a symbol of the Christian religion.

cycle An order of events that are repeated again and again.

Eucharist A ceremony in which people eat bread and drink wine in memory of the last meal Jesus ate with his followers.

fast To go without food for religious reasons.

First Holy Communion A Roman Catholic ceremony. It is the first time that a young person takes Holy Communion, usually when he or she is about seven or eight years old.

godparents People close to the child's family who promise at the baptism to teach the child about the Christian religion as he or she grows up.

Holy Communion The Roman Catholic form of the Eucharist ceremony, when people eat bread and drink wine in memory of the last meal Jesus ate with his followers.

Holy Spirit The power of God in the world. It helps people to do what God wants.

Holy Trinity The unity of God (the Father), Jesus (the Son) and the Holy Spirit, which together are one God.

Holy Week The week before Easter Sunday.

Last Supper The last meal that Jesus shared with his followers before his arrest and death.

lectern The stand that holds the Bible or notes for the minister's sermon.

Lent The season of 40 days before Easter (not including Sundays). Some Christians give up favourite foods or things they enjoy to remember Jesus' suffering.

Mass A Roman Catholic ceremony to remember the last meal Christ had with his followers.

minister A trained religious leader. In the Catholic church and the Church of England, the minister is usually called a priest.

Orthodox Christians Churches such as the Russian and Greek Church. They are sometimes called the Eastern Churches.

Passover A Jewish holiday when people remember how the Jews were freed from slavery in Egypt.

persecuted When people are treated cruelly and unfairly because of their race, religion or political beliefs. The early Christians were persecuted because of their religion.

pulpit A stand where the minister stands to give the sermon.

Saviour A name for Jesus. It means someone who saves people from danger.

Shrove Tuesday The day before the beginning of Lent. It is traditional to eat pancakes to use up eggs and fat, which cannot be eaten during Lent.

symbolise To be a symbol for.

Whitsun (also called Pentecost) A festival 50 days after Easter Sunday. People remember the coming of the Holy Spirit, which helped Jesus' followers spread his teachings.

✝ Further information

Books to read

I Belong To the Christian Faith by Katie Dicker and Sam Dilkes (Wayland, 2008)

My Bible Story Book by Carine Mackenzie (Christian Focus Publications Ltd, 2007)

Religious Articles: Objects used in Worship by Anita Ganeri (Steck-Vaughn, 2000)

Stories Jesus Told: Favorite Stories from the Bible by Nick Butterworth (Candle Books, 2005)

Websites for children

Christian symbols
http://atschool.eduweb.co.uk/carolrb/hinduism/hindui.html

Christian crafts
http://www.eggventurebeads.com/pdfs/palm_tribal.pdf
Simple instructions for making palm crosses

RE online for Juniors
http://juniors.reonline.org.uk/topiclist.php?20
Christianity: What do signs and symbols mean in religion? (KS2)

Re online
http://www.reonline.org.uk/allre/tt_links.php?191
KS3 Symbolism

Note to parents and teachers: Every effort has been made by the publishers to ensure that these websites are suitable for children. However, because of the nature of the Internet, it is impossible to guarantee that the contents of these sites will not be altered. We strongly advise that Internet access is supervised by a responsible adult.

Teachers' resources

Inside a Catholic Church: A Guide to Signs, Symbols and Saints by Joseph M. Champlin (Abingdon Press, 2003)

Rings, Kings and Butterflies: Lessons on Christian Symbols for Children by Harriet Vandermeer (Augsburg Fortress, 2006)

Teacher Resource Exchange
http://tre.ngfl.gov.uk/server.php?request=cmVzb3VyY2UuZnVsbHZpZXc=&resourceId=11439
Christian symbols: includes details of some Christian symbols and an activity.

Places to visit

For virtual tours of different kinds of churches, go to
http://juniors.reonline.org.uk/juniors_vtours.php?c

For information and advice about visiting different types of churches in the UK, go to
http://pow.reonline.org.uk/
Places of Worship: Christianity

✝ Index